I0789621

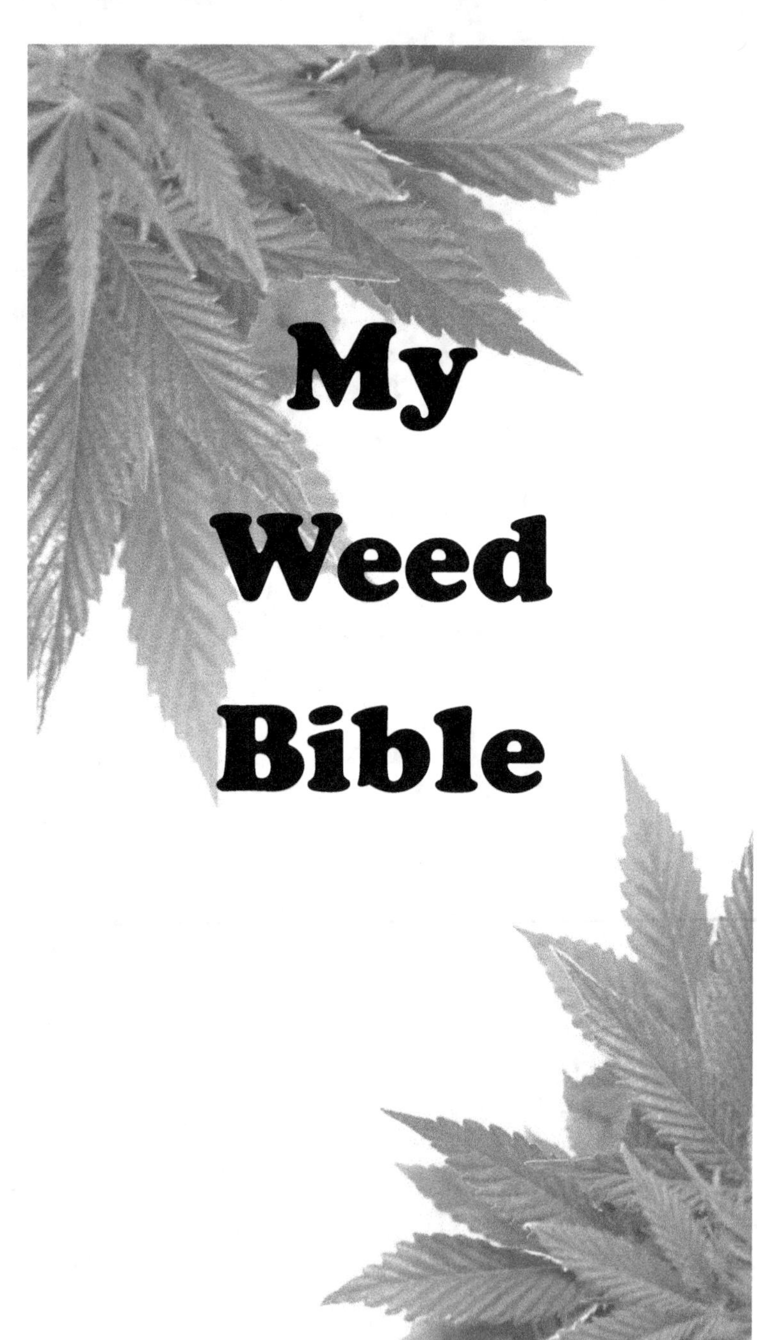

My Weed Bible

This book is intended for all of ages (no minors) people to learn how to enjoy cannabis .

In no way am I telling you what to do , I am just showing you many options to enjoy .

I do encourage you to do your own home work on any purchase or decision .

I hope you enjoy my book as much as I enjoyed making it .

The world is huge & the possibilities are endless !!

For a
Stoner
From a
Stoner

INHALE

EXHALE

She was free !! Free from being hated , scorned upon . After so many years of hate propaganda . Finally she could breath and be herself .

She had been around since the beginning of time . 10 , 000 years to guess . She had fed people , made cloths for them & even helped as a medicine healer .

So natural she could never understand why anyone could ever hate her .

Her name was

MARYJANE

Cannabis,

also known as marijuana

(MARY JANE)

among other names, is a

psychoactive drug from the

Cannabis plant used primarily for

medical or

recreational purpose.

Cannabis was legalized in Canada October 17th 2018 .

Countries that have legalized recreational cannabis use are Canada, Georgia, South Africa, and Uruguay, plus 15 states, 2 territories, and the District of Columbia in the United States and the Australian Capital Territory in Australia.

Commercial cannabis production and sale is legal nationwide in two countries (Canada and Uruguay) and in all subnational U.S. jurisdictions that have legalized cannabis except Washington, D.C.

Ok its legal ...
Now what ?

LETS GET

HIGH !!!

Everything you need
to know about
Cannabis
plus more

Benefits of smoking Cannabis

Cannabis can actually improve lung function.

A study in the journal Obesity found that regular weed smokers are less likely to be obese than non-smokers.

Marijuana can make people more creative .

Studies have shown that cannabis has an anti-inflammatory effect, which is one reason why medical marijuana works so well .

Cannabis can kill cancer cells.

Anxiety

Cannabis has anti-anxiety properties, which can help people with disorders .

What is more, there are clearly people who can function well, extremely well, while high on Cannabis .

However this is not a one size fits all situation . Some people who use cannabis experience anxiety.

Most find using cannabis to unwind after a stressful day calm & relaxing .

420

420 is April 20th
(4th month 20 day)
considered as an
occasion for smoking or
celebrating the smoking
of marijuana.

Every year
All around the world.

Ways to Bust up Your Cannabis

1) Cut up with scissors

2) Use a coffee grinder

3) Use a shot glass (fill up half way) and use scissors to chop

4) Use a pill bottle & a coin . Fill bottle up half way , drop a coin in , secure lid & shake for approx. 2 mins

5) Buy a grinder

6) Use a knife (be careful!!)

7) If all else fails use your fingers

Rolling Papers

Now this is up to you . Mostly trial and error until you find a paper you like rolling with .

I personally prefer zig-zag blues (some would call them horse paper lol) But I find they do well with the variety of cannabis I smoke . Again this is your choice , so have fun . Try different papers ! You might be surprised at what your favorite is .

PIPES

Cannabis pipes are the easiest tools to use. Pipes are affordable & timeless.

Cannabis & Tobacco pipes are the same

Simple to use , you grind your weed , place in pipe , watch how you position your lighter & place your finger over the carb (the little hole) , inhale

& exhale . Be sure & take your mouth off the pipe before exhaling as this will cause your weed to fly out of the pipe !

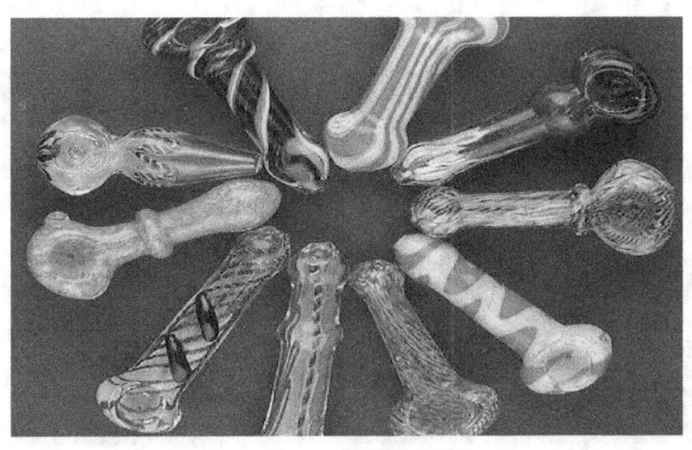

Rolling a joint is a must have skill for anyone who wants to smoke cannabis.

Knowing how to roll a joint will help you so much for the long haul. .

It will also make sure that you don't waste any of your precious Cannabis.

PACKING THE PAPER

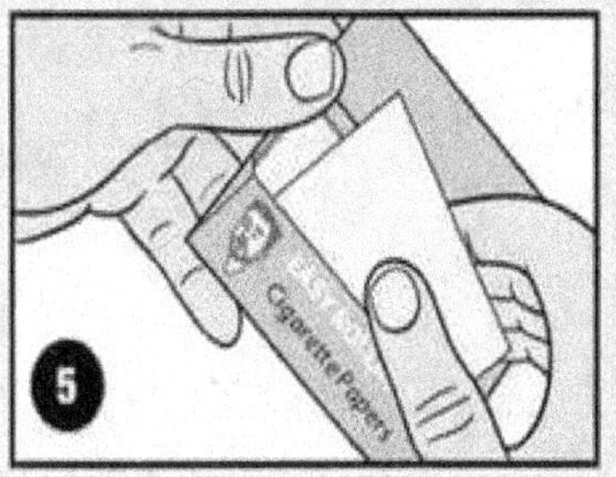

Grab your favorite rolling papers.

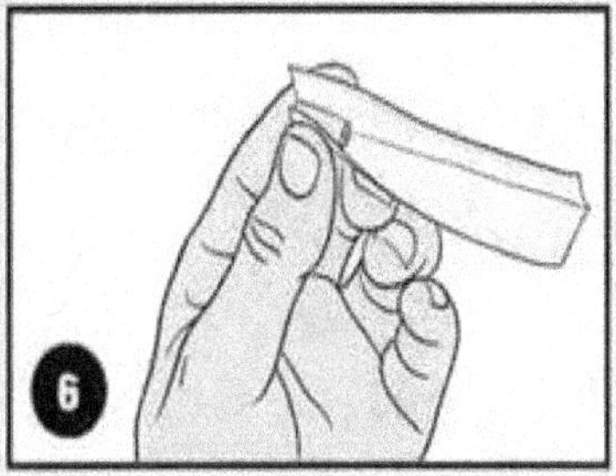

Place tightly wrapped filter at end of paper.

Hold the filter end with your thumb and index finger.

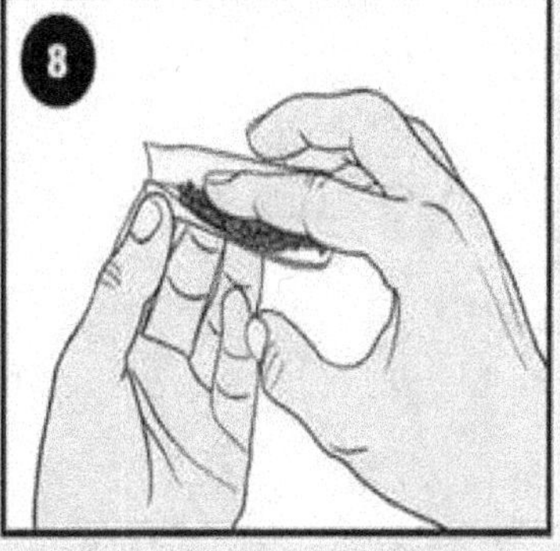

Add your favorite ground bud and level with filter width.

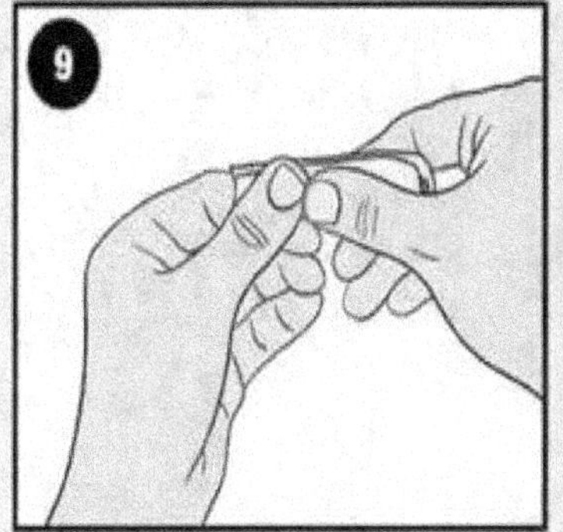

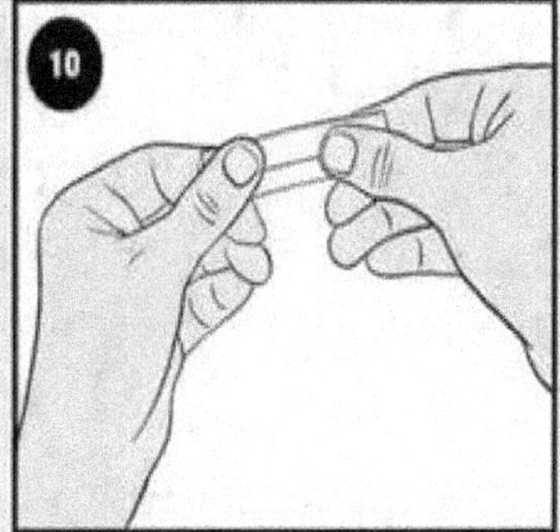

Pinch together the papers and begin to roll in an up and down motion.

Rolling Machines

No shame in purchasing a rolling machine .

Took me foreverrrrrrrrr to roll a proper joint .

Again SO many to choose from

Have fun in picking your new best friend.

What is a Filter ?

A filter ensures a cleaner and better-tasting joint (no weed falling out of the end)

The handmade weed filter used is simply cardstock folded origami-style.

Airflow is increased through this filter which clears the passageway for the smoke to travel within the joint paper, & the way it's folded keeps the joint from collapsing .

Blunts

A blunt is a cigar that has been hollowed out and filled with cannabis.

It is rolled with the tobacco -leaf "wrap", usually from an inexpen- sive cigar .

How to Roll a Blunt

You need to open up that cigar.

Gut the cigar.

Pack that blunt.

This is the messy part.

Roll up that fatty.

Lick & Seal .

(if it wont stick use other rolling papers to help ...)

Practice Makes Perfect

(I still have problems rolling blunts ... thank gawd for friends)

Roach Clip

Roach clip is the unofficial name for any tool that helps you smoke and pass a small joint/blunt .

Most roach clips you simply have to clamp down to open the clip, then you close it onto the end of the joint (roach end) .

Keeps your fingers from picking up the smell & getting burnt.

Vaporizers

Vaporizing heats the bud to the point where the THC is turned into vapor rather than smoke, resulting in a cleaner, healthier method of getting high . There are arguments as to if this is such a healthier way to smoke cannabis , again it is a personal choice .

BONG LIFE

This is a must know in the Pot World

Bongs do 2 things :

1) Cools down the pot smoke

2) It cleans the pot smoke (pretty darn cool)

The reservoir of water helps

dissipate the heat of the smoke.

The result is smoke with a much lower temperature.

(It gets even cooler if you're using ice … there are also freezer bongs)

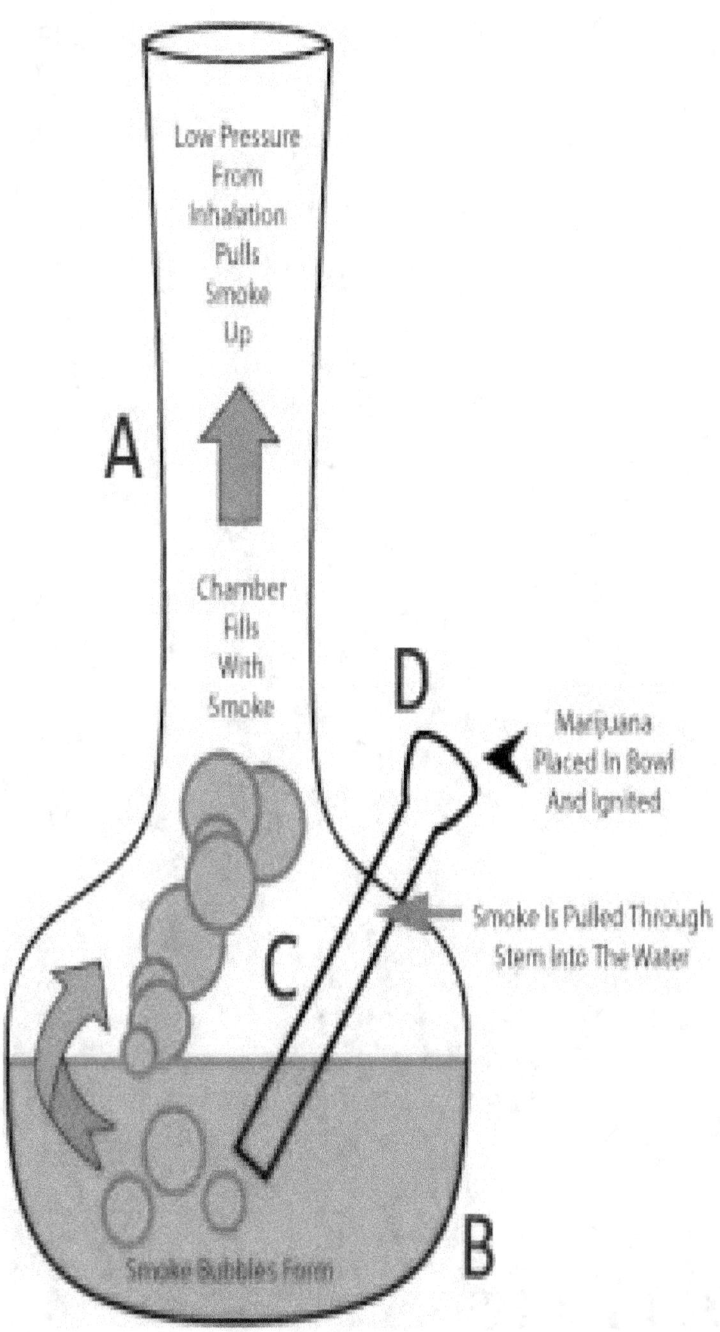

Low Pressure From Inhalation Pulls Smoke Up
A
Chamber Fills With Smoke
D
Marijuana Placed In Bowl And Ignited
C
Smoke Is Pulled Through Stem Into The Water
Smoke Bubbles Form
B

Gravity Bong

A gravity bong typically consists of cut up plastic bottles , an aluminum foil bowl & a container of water .

This works on suction .

(science , eh ?)

Sativa , Indica or Hybrid ?

Sativa : Sativa is the strain of cannabis that makes you laugh and gives you an active head high .

Indica : Indica strains of marijuana are known for their relaxing, therapeutic qualities and for providing chronic pain relief .

Hybrid : Hybrid cannabis plants are a combination of indica and sativa strains .

The record
for the
Worlds
LARGEST JOINT
had
100 grams
of weed
in it

Hot Knifes

The "hot knives" method is among the oldest and most popular ways to smoke cannabis.

you heat up the knife by placing it on your heating element, like an electric stove, gas heater, or hot plate. Once the knife is hot you dab some weed onto it and inhale.

Using a half a plastic bottle, a straw, or even a funnel will catch more of the smoke . Less Waste.

I AM TO BUSY WORKING ON MY GRASS TO NOTICE IF YOURS IS GREENER

One Hitter

A one hitter is a small pipe with a narrow bowl that is designed and used for a single inhalation (one hit)

Apple Pipe

Making an Apple Pipe Using a Pen Get an apple and a pen. Remove the stem from the apple. Bore a hole through the top of the apple. Bore a second hole near the bottom of the apple. Bore a third hole on the side of the apple. Make a bowl. Use the pipe.

This procedure can be applied to many different fruits !!

Weights

A gram is one gram

An eighth = 3.5 grams.

A quarter = 7 grams

A half = 14 grams

An ounce = 28 grams

A pound = 448 grams

A kilogram = 1000 grams

A Friend With Weed is a Friend Indeed

Why Buy a Scale ?

Knowing just how much you smoke is important for these reasons .

You won't accidentally get shorted by your dealer \ dispensary

You will have a better understanding of the basic

 cannabis measurements

For patients who are prescribed cannabis , it's even more critical to know just how much you are

 using.

Knowing how to weigh weed will help you a lot in the future .

Dabs

Dabs are a type of marijuana extract. There are many different types of dabs available , the most common being shatter , budder & hash oil .

Dabs often look like a thin sheet of glass like substance . You use vaporizers or dab rigs to smoke it .

Bible ?

Does the Bible address the use of marijuana?

Yes and No!

Some believe it is explicitly endorsed in Genesis 1:29

"Behold, I have given you every plant yielding seed that is on the face of all the earth, and every tree with seed in its fruit. You shall have them for food."

Again that is your decision on how you want to perceive the information !

Slang names for Consuming Cannabis

420	Blaze
Session	Toke
Wake & Bake	Get Baked
Tea Party	Safety Meeting
Burn One	Torch Up
Get High	Hotbox
Get Stoned	Clam bake

Fire in the Hole

THIS

IS

HOW

I

ROLL

Slang for How Cannabis makes you Feel

Cottonmouth	Fried
High	Stoned
Toasted	Baked
Buzzed	Lit Up
Munchies	Wasted
Couchlock	Zooted
Natures Holiday	Smacked

Cbd oil

(CBD) is a cannabinoid – a chemical compound that acts throughout the body, including on certain parts of the brain.

Cannabidiol is a popular natural remedy used for many common ailments , to list s few …

cluster and other headaches

post-traumatic stress disorder (PTSD)

cancer

allergies or asthma

epilepsy and other seizure disorders

multiple sclerosis (MS)

lung conditions

Alzheimer's disease

Edibles

Offering a tasty alternative to smoking or vaporizing cannabis, Edible forms of cannabis, including food

products, lozenges, and capsules, can produce effective, long-lasting, and safe effects .

Please be careful and start out with lower amounts !

Slang names for Cannabis

Mary Jane	Gunga
Lobo	Bud
Devils Lettuce	Green
Chloe	Dank
Reefer	Pot
Kief	Jolly
Spliff	Dew
Cheeba	Flower
Greta	Grass
Cabbage	Sticky Icky

In a relationship with

Cannabis

It's Not Complicated

Buy or grow

Now again this is your choice .

If you feel like you have a green thumb & some cash to spend then try growing . It does require a lot of time & sometimes trial and error to find a system that works for you .

However if you are like most of us out there , you can find a reliable source and be happy with that .

A local dealer or a government store will be able to help you . Ask around , other stoners are very helpful .

THE ABC's ......

A is for Alligator Cigarette

B is for Blunt

C is for Chronic

D is for Dank

E is for Eighth

F is for Flower

G is for Ganja

H is for Herb

I is for Indica

J is for Joint

K is for Kief

L is for Leaf

M is for Mary Jane

N is for Nug

O is for Ounce

P is for Pot

Q is for Quarter

R is for Resin

S is for Stash

T is for THC

U is for U (smoke dat weed)

V is for Volcano

W is for Whacky Tabacky

X is for hey … don't share this with
your x !!

Y is for You .. Please see U

And …….

Z is for Zoo Wee MaMa

WHEN
YOU
SAID
FRIENDS
WITH
BENEFITS
i ASSUMED
YOU HAD WEED

Slang names for GROSS cannabis

Brown	Garbage
Swag	Whack
Harsh	Firewood
Ditch Weed	Cabbage
Bush Weed	Dirt Grass
Bobby	Shake
Swag	Leaf
Rip OFF	POO

Cannabis was used as a truth serum by the US government during WW11

PUFF

PUFF

PASS

Hash

Hash is a concentrated form of cannabis made made by compressing and processing trichomes of the cannabis plant. Smoke it in a joint , bong , pipe , hot knifes … your choice !

Slang names for GREAT Cannabis

Bc bud	Nug
Primo	Colas
Dank	Hydro
Good Stuff	Gas
Chiba Chiba	Chronic
Za za	Killer Green Bud
Flower Tops	Killa
Citrol	Buddha
Golden Leaf	Nug

Songs That Mention Cannabis

La Cucaracha

Smoke Two Joints - Toyes

Roll Another # - Neil Young

Big Spliff — Murphys Law

Smoke Some Pot — Dash Rip Rock

How to roll a blunt - Redman

Mary Jane — Rick James

Sweet Leaf — Black Sabbath

Legalize it — Peter Tosh

Overdose ?

It is **IMPOSSIBLE** to overdose
on cannabis ,

However you could

GREEN

out from

smoking to much .

Green out :

room spinning , puking or

passing out.

Munchies

The active ingredient THC inhibits a cannabinoid receptor known as CB1 .

This receptor is also involved in signaling the appetite — supressing hormone Leptin .

When CBI is blocked Leptin doesn't get activated.

And this is why you may experience the Munchies .

Beer

Beers hops are in the
same family of flowering plants as
cannabis.

That would make

beer & cannabis cousins!!

Difference Between Hemp & Cannabis

Cannabis and hemp plants contain both CBD and THC along with more than 540 other substances. The main difference between the two plants is the amount of each compound they contain. Cannabis contains more THC, and less CBD.

Hemp contains more CBD and less THC

The Presidents

7 of the earliest presidents were well known as hemp smokers:

George Washington, Thomas Jefferson, James Madison, James Monroe, Andrew Jackson, Zachary Taylor and Franklin Pierce .

Not only did they speak great things of the plant, some of these presidents were a huge part in the creation of a hemp industry.

Be

DOPE.

different. original. peaceful. extraordinary

Kief

(Hippy Crack)

Kief is the resinous trichomes of cannabis that may accumulate in containers or be sifted from loose, dry cannabis grinders with a mesh screen .Collected and used for thousands of years as a way to consume cannabis .

There are many grinders available for collecting kief .

You can scrap the side of your grinder to collect kief and save it … press it … smoke it … options

I throw it in my joints for a extra high .

Wet Cannabis

If you have purchased wet weed , don't smoke it that way ! It will have a funny taste ,

be hard to light and be way less

 enjoyable . Not to mention if it has been wet for a period of time it may have mold spores (they do not go away with drying)

If you smoke moldy weed the spores can settle into your lungs and grow large mold balls, which are hard to get rid of and

sometimes have to be removed Surgically.

Cannabis Mold

Now don't freak out !

But it is good to be smart &
know some ways of telling if
your cannabis has mold .

How to Check :

smells moldy, urine-ish, catty

black or dark green spots

black light test - mold glows green

grey green cotton candy mold is
the most common

Ways to dry your cannabis

(fresh cut , not moldy)

In the sun ! Use nature !

Blow dryer on low

Use your oven (180 F) door open on a baking tray , be careful !

Well ventilated area (top of the fridge)

Hang it up !

If at all possible avoid buying wet cannabis !

Dry Cannabis

Ok here is the opposite problem . Your weed is as dry as a popcorn fart . That's no fun .

You will be smoking sawdust . You can moisten up your

cannabis by :

putting a piece of bread , cut up piece of potatoe , orange peels , a damp paper towel & even apple slices into the same bag as your cannabis . Keep it to the other side of the bag and close up . It will refresh your supply !!

CANNABIS

is the most

WIDELY

used

DRUG

in the

WORLD

Famous People Who smoke Cannabis

Lady Gaga	Bob Dylan
Snoop Dogg	Carl Sagan
Bill Maher	Rihanna
Jay Z	Zayn Malik
Hugh Hefner	Bob Marley
Drake	Miley Cyrus
Jimi Hendrix	Lil Wayne
Brad Pitt	Cameron Diaz
The Beetles	Roseanne

Smell

Cannabis can come with a lingering smell .

You can help get rid of this smell by smoking outdoors or in a well ventilated area .

If smoking indoors you can try these methods :

Have a window open

Use a fan to exhaust smell

Incense

Air fresheners

Burn a candle

Air Purifiers

Storage

The best way to store your Cannabis is by using airtight glass jars .

They keep your weed safe from the moisture , air and keeps the smell in .

This also helps keep your cannabis stay fresh longer.

My Weed Notes

HAPPY
420

Other Titles By Linda Larson

Jewels of Italy 2020

British Columbia Day Dreaming

Verona Romeo & Juliet

Valentine Ideas for Everybody

Bible jokes for kids

God's Love

Fun , Easy & Affordable ideas

Follow me on Instagram

Facebook & Amazon

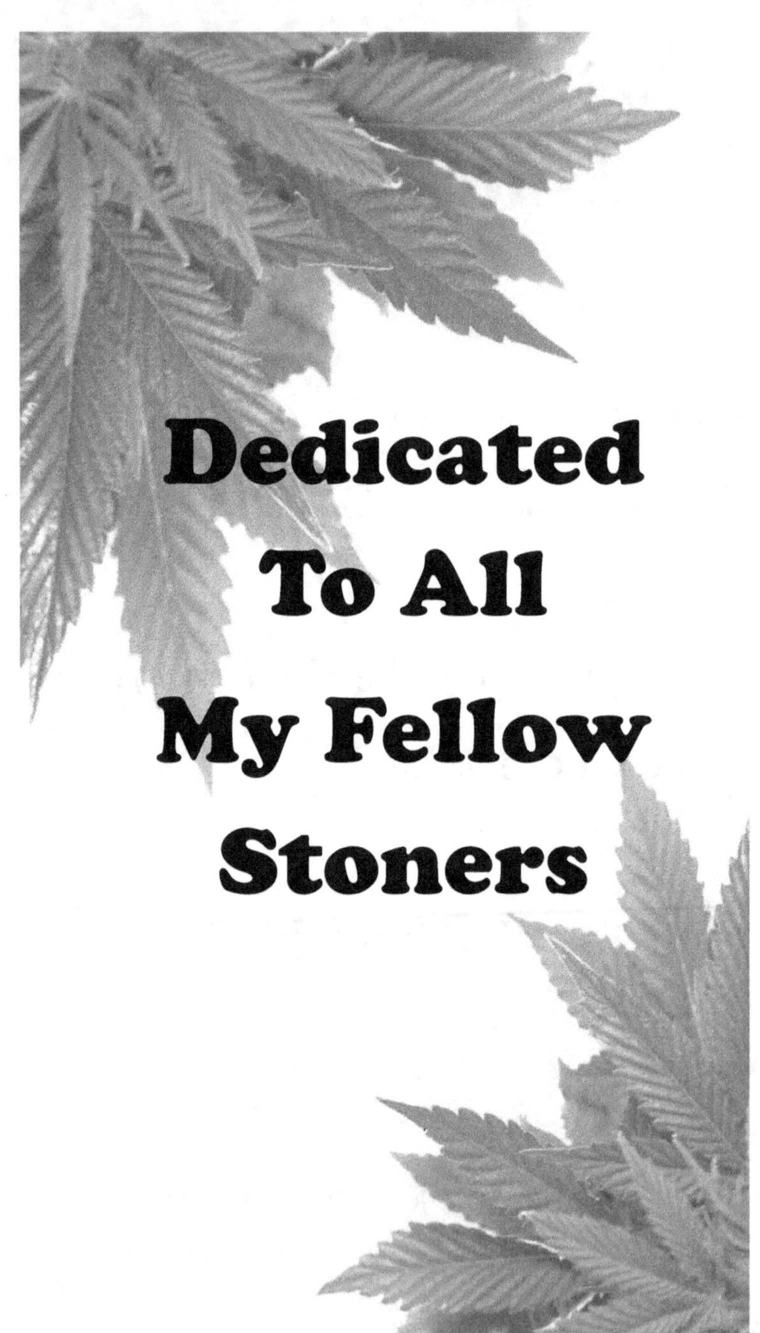

Dedicated
To All
My Fellow
Stoners

Peace , Love & Weed

Linda Larson